THE HEYDAY OF THE TROLLEYBUS - 2

Geoff Lumb

IAN ALLAN Publishing

Front cover: For 30 years, between 28 March 1938 and 12 May 1968, trolleybuses could be seen in Belfast. After a mixture of 14 trial vehicles, a fleet of 114 AEC type 664T trolleybuses with GEC equipment was ordered. Due to the war, the Ministry of War Transport would allow only 88 to be built, these arriving between 1940 and 1943. A further 14 utility two-axle Sunbeam W4 vehicles were also allocated. After the war, Belfast ordered 70 three-axle trolleybuses with GEC equipment from Guy Motors, and 24 of the BUT type 9641T, all with bodies built by Harkness on Park Royal frames. This view shows Guy No 153, AEC No 19 and BUT No 208 on a summer afternoon at Bellevue turning circle on the Antrim Road in July 1963. Guy No 153 was new in January 1949, AEC No 19 was new in June 1941 and BUT No 208 was new in October 1950.
V. Nutton, courtesy Geoff Lumb collection

Back cover: Huddersfield purchased two batches of BUT type 9641T trolleybuses, fitted with East Lancashire Coachbuilders 72-seat bodies, in 1954 and 1956. One of the first batch, No 613, is seen at Lockwood Bar in 1965, returning from Lockwood Church to Huddersfield and Brackenhall. The tram route beyond Lockwood to Honley was not converted to trolleybuses in 1939 due to the low bridge in Woodhead Road. *G. Lumb*

Title page: The Mexborough & Swinton postwar fleet replacements comprised 33 Sunbeam model W4 and F4, Brush 32-seat centre-entrance-bodied trolleybuses which entered service between 1947 and 1950. Typical of these was No 26 (FWX 910) which is seen unloading in Mexborough. The last M&S trolleybus ran on 26 March 1961, and in 1968 the company's routes and motorbuses were absorbed into the fleet of Yorkshire Traction. *R. Brook*

Introduction

This is a companion volume to the highly successful colour album *Heyday of the Trolleybus*, published two years ago.

The trolleybus was a hybrid vehicle introduced to Britain in 1909, with the first examples entering service in Leeds and Bradford in 1911 on feeder routes to the existing tramway systems where the potential receipts did not justify the cost of building tramway extensions.

The trolleybus was similar to a motorbus but instead of a petrol engine to drive the vehicle, an electric motor was used. The power for this was obtained from two overhead wires which carried the 500–600V dc electric supply, with one wire being the positive supply and the other the negative return.

First published 1996

ISBN 0 7110 2463 4

© Ian Allan Ltd 1996

Published by Ian Allan Publishing

an imprint of Ian Allan Ltd,
Terminal House, Station Approach,
Shepperton, Surrey TW17 8AS.
Printed by Ian Allan Printing Ltd,
Coombelands House, Coombelands Lane,
Addlestone, Surrey KT15 1HY.

Between 1911 and April 1949 when the last trolleybus system was built, 50 municipalities or companies had operated trolleybuses, not all concurrently. Trolleybuses continued to be used until March 1972 when the last British operator withdrew them from its remaining route. Bradford has the distinction of being the operator who used trolleybuses for 61 years — longer than anybody else in Britain; on the other hand, the first operator to abandon its trolleybuses was Dundee, which after only 20 months' use withdrew them in May 1914.

The demand for trolleybuses peaked in 1937 with 24 examples, some in chassis form and some with bodies, being displayed by 14 chassis and body builders at the 1937 Commercial Motor Show. In May 1939 when Brighton Corporation replaced its tramway system with trolleybuses, it became the 47th operator to introduce them.

By the time World War 2 started in September 1939, 12 of the 47 operators had already decided that the trolleybus was not the solution to their transport problems and had withdrawn them. The usual changeover from tram to trolleybus operation was more or less halted by the war, with only three more systems introducing them: Cardiff in 1942, Brighton, Hove & District in 1946, after its vehicles had been stored for the duration of the hostilities; and finally Glasgow in April 1949, which became the last operator to introduce trolleybuses.

The nationalisation of the electricity supply industry after the war in 1947/48 forced many operators to pay more for the electric power, and then after the backlog of postwar orders was completed, the whole transport industry went into a steady decline when the social habits of passengers changed. The advent of television, with its spell-binding attraction, caused a rapid fall in evening travel which affected cinemas and theatres, many of which closed. Reducing the frequencies at off-peak times became the norm, but with trolleybus operation it meant that the fixed costs had to be spread over fewer vehicles and journeys, resulting in costs per mile increasing. With the financial returns decreasing, many operators found that they could not afford to purchase new trolleybuses, which due to the reduced demand were costing more to produce, so the number of manufacturers was reduced to two in 1951. To many operators, therefore, the only solution was to abandon their operations and substitute the cheaper motorbus. Birmingham was the first postwar operator to withdraw its small fleet of trolleybuses from its two routes and replace them with the more flexible motorbus.

The biggest user of trolleybuses in Britain was London Transport, whose postwar fleet consisted of 1,800 vehicles built between 1935 and 1952. In 1954 it had been decided to replace these by motorbuses, so that between 1959 and May 1962, London's trolleybuses disappeared. In late 1960 the other 24 operators still using trolleybuses were operating 1,975 vehicles between them. Thus the heyday of the trolleybus is unquestionably the period between 1937 and 1960.

After this only 29 new trolleybuses entered service in Britain: eight at Derby in 1960; 12 at Reading in 1961, six of which were fitted with refurbished motors and electrical equipment from withdrawn Reading trolleybuses; and then in 1962, nine Sunbeams at Bournemouth became the last new ones in Britain. Bradford continued to place second-hand trolleybuses into service in 1960/61, and then in 1962/63 it placed 12 rebuilt vehicles into service: five ex-Doncaster but originally Darlington BUTs and seven ex-Mexborough & Swinton Sunbeam F4 trolleybuses which were all fitted with East Lancs 66-seat forward-entrance bodies. After this the only other developments were existing chassis fitted with new bodies at Huddersfield, Maidstone, Teesside and Wolverhampton.

Walsall placed 14 secondhand trolleybuses into service in 1961/62, with three of these being rebuilt and lengthened to become 67/69-seat forward entrance vehicles. During 1962 Huddersfield cancelled the order for new bodies for the last four refurbished chassis; instead it fitted four earlier bodies built in 1955/56 from vehicles needing chassis overhaul. The last trolleybus was rebodied in 1965 when the last of the seven 1950 Sunbeam F4 trolleybuses to be fitted with new Roe 61-seat bodies entered service at Teesside.

The photographs in this album have been selected to give the reader a pictorial glimpse of as many of the 50 trolleybus operators as possible, presenting them in chronological order of the closure of their systems. Unfortunately colour film was not readily available commercially when many of the first 12 systems closed between 1914 and 1938. However, the 38 systems operating since World War 2 have been reasonably well covered by many well-known photographers to whom I am very grateful for willingly making available many of the 'gems' which are included in my selection. My only regret is that I could not include all of them but, who knows, there might be an opportunity later. I have not been able to cover every type or model of trolleybus built, but hope that the reader enjoys these glimpses of a vehicle which was so successful in providing a smooth and silent form of transport in contrast to the rival contemporary motorbus which was slow and noisy.

As author of the book *British Trolleybuses 1911–1972,* published in 1995 by Ian Allan Ltd, about the manufacturers, I hope that readers, many of whom have never experienced travel by trolleybus, will enjoy this opportunity to see examples in colour from many of the suppliers whose products revolutionised local transport so many years ago, when the private car was available to only a few, and municipal pride played an important role in providing the best form of transport for its residents, until economics dictated otherwise.

Geoff Lumb
Huddersfield
February 1996

Acknowledgements

I would like to thank the following for allowing me access to their photographic collections: Roy Brook, C. Carter, V. Nutton, A. Richardson (Photobus) D. J. Smithies and G. R. Marshall. And finally, grateful thanks to my wife Ethel for translating scribbled notes into legible captions on disk. Without their help this interpretation of the British trolleybus would not have been possible.

Keighley

Above: Keighley Corporation ceased to operate trolleybuses on 31 August 1932. A few days before, a joint company — Keighley–West Yorkshire Services Ltd — was formed to co-ordinate services previously operated by Keighley Corporation and the West Yorkshire Road Car Co in Keighley and district, using motorbuses. One of the displaced trolleybuses which had been in use as a caravan was rescued for preservation in the late 1960s and was then kept at Peter Black's car museum in Keighley until 1994 when it was moved to the Bradford Industrial Museum. Its original crimson and white livery was obscured by green paint whilst in use as a caravan. Our view shows No 5 (WT 7105) in March 1964. New in November 1924, No 5 was one of 10 Brush-bodied 50-seat double-deck 'Straker-Clough' trolley omnibuses supplied by Clough Smith & Co, the cost being £2,020 each when new. *G. Lumb*

Birmingham

Below: Birmingham introduced trolleybuses on the Nechells route in 1922 using 12 Roe-bodied double-deckers very similar in appearance to the Keighley one. In 1934 a second route was opened from Yardley to two different termini in the city centre, again replacing trams, using 50 Leyland three-axle model TTBD2 trolleybuses with locally manufactured GEC electrical equipment and MCW-built 58-seat bodies. One of these, No 31 (OC 1131), is seen on a warm day in Moor Street in 1949. Trolleybuses were withdrawn in 1941 from the Nechells route and in 1951 from Yardley and its later extensions. *C. Carter*

Llanelly

Left: One of the few company-owned trolleybus systems was Llanelly & District Traction Co which was one of the Balfour Beatty & Co Ltd subsidiaries. Trolleybuses had replaced trams on Boxing Day 1932 using the first seven of the 14 Leyland TBD2 vehicles to be delivered. These were the first trolleybuses to be ordered from Leyland Motors Ltd, the previous ones being supplied by GEC with Leyland as the sub-contractor. No 4 (TH 3007) is seen in 1951 at Town Hall, Llanelly on route 1 to Loughor. The condition of the 50-seat Leyland body reminds us that at this time the ownership of L&DT Co was in the hands of the South Wales electricity board who had taken over the company in 1948 when the electricity supply companies were nationalised. *C. Carter*

Above: In 1952 the trolleybus undertaking was sold to the South Wales Transport Co which within nine months closed the system in November 1952. During World War 2, 12 utility-bodied Karrier W4 trolleybuses were allocated, the last six arriving in 1946 having bodies built by Park Royal. Three of these are seen outside Llanelly station in 1951, No 44 (CBX 910) being the front vehicle. After the closure of Llanelly, two complete 1945 utility Roe-bodied trolleybuses were sold to Maidstone, with the chassis of the other 10 going to Bradford which rebuilt them and fitted them with new East Lancs bodies before placing them in service. *C. Carter*

7

West Hartlepool

Above: The original fleet of trolleybuses introduced between 1924 and 1927 was replaced by West Hartlepool Corporation in 1938/39 when 14 Daimler CTM4 trolleybuses with Roe 54-seat double-deck bodies and three 32-seat single-deck Roe centre-entrance bodied Leyland TB7 trolleybuses arrived. Eight of the Daimlers were jointly owned by both West Hartlepool and Hartlepool Corporations and were used on the route connecting the two adjacent towns, being operated, by arrangement, by West Hartlepool. One of the jointly owned trolleybuses, No 33 (EF 6893), is seen in 1951 outside the bus station in West Hartlepool in pouring rain with the nearside windscreen open (to avoid condensation?); a lovely atmospheric shot. This was the last route to close, on 2 April 1953. The author remembers seeing all the last nine West Hartlepool and the eight jointly owned trolleybuses in a scrapyard at Thornaby in July 1953. *C. Carter*

Notts & Derby

Above: Another Balfour Beatty & Co Ltd subsidiary company was the Nottingham & Derbyshire Traction Co (Notts & Derby) which operated trolleybuses linking Ripley with Nottingham some 14½ miles away, as well as an eight-mile route linking Heanor with Hallamfields. The original 1932/33 fleet was replaced between 1937 and 1949 by AEC type 661T and BUT 9611T two-axle double-deckers with 56-seat Weymann bodies. In 1948 ownership was transferred to the British Electricity Authority, and then in 1949 the British Transport Commission became responsible for the system, eventually linking it to the Midland General bus operations. The system was abandoned in April 1953, with all the trolleybuses being sold to Bradford for further use. No 353, one of the last batch of 15 Weymann-bodied BUT 9611T trolleybuses, is seen in 1951 turning in Nottingham, King Street before returning on route A1 to Ripley. *C. Carter*

Southend

Below: Southend Corporation operated trolleybuses between 1925 and 1954 initially using single-deck vehicles. The first double-deck trolleybuses arrived in 1928/29 when six Garrett three-axle models were placed into service. In 1932 a batch of four AEC 661T trolleybuses with lowbridge 48-seat bodies built by English Electric at Preston were placed into service. A further five similar trolleybuses arrived in 1933. One of the first batch, No 113 is seen in 1949 in South Church Avenue and still carries the English Electric winged motif in addition to the AEC triangular badge. *C. Carter*

The author apologises for the lack of sharpness in this view, which has been included to illustrate the style introduced in 1932 for the first AEC/EE trolleybuses to be built. In this design a false radiator was included to give access to the traction control equipment. By late 1933 this style was obsolete and thus this view is of great historical significance.

Many of these early views have had to be reproduced from 35mm duplicates made from fragile Dufay colour film originals. Some of these originals were taken more than 47 years ago when colour film was in its infancy and when the quality of materials varied, making it difficult to photograph moving vehicles without some loss of sharpness as a result of limits to the depth of field when using slow film stock.

Above: In 1946 five secondhand single-deck trolleybuses, new in 1936 to the Teesside Railless Traction Board, were purchased for £250 each from W. North, the Leeds dealer. These carried 32-seat rear-entrance bodies built by Massey Bros, one of the Wigan body builders. The chassis supplied by Leyland Motors was model TB3 with GEC equipment. One of these five, No 142, is seen at Kursaal in 1949.
C. Carter

Pontypridd

Above: Pontypridd Urban District Council introduced trolleybuses on its only route linking Cilfynydd to Treforest some 3.3 miles away, in 1930. This cross-town route used seven single-deck English Electric-built trolleybuses, and then Pontypridd became the proud owner of two double-deck trolleybuses originally built as demonstrators for Guy Motors and the Bristol Tramways & Carriage Co Ltd. During World War 2 eight utility-bodied Karrier W4 trolleybuses arrived: four with Park Royal bodies, with Roe and Weymann each supplying two bodies. When Pontypridd withdrew its trolleybuses in January 1957 it was the last system to use trolley-wheel collectors instead of the more modern sliding shoes. It was also the last Urban District Council to operate trolleybuses (the other UDCs to operate trolleybuses were Aberdare and Ramsbottom).

The eight trolleybuses were purchased by Doncaster (two), South Shields (four) and Walsall (two). No 14 was one of the two Roe-bodied ones sold to Walsall before closure in 1956, and it is seen at Broadway in 1952, with one of Rhondda's AEC motorbuses behind the British Railways Scammell mechanical horse delivering goods from the railway station — also a reminder that the railway was once a common carrier before Dr Beeching. *C. Carter*

Darlington

Below: Darlington Corporation was another operator to abandon trolleybuses in 1957, when it withdrew its last eight vehicles. Trolleybuses had been introduced in 1925 and all vehicles except the six purchased in 1949 were centre-entrance single-deck ones. The odd six were East Lancs 56-seat double-deckers on BUT type 9611T chassis which were used only until 1952 when they were sold to Doncaster, another town on the A1 Great North trunk road linking London with Edinburgh. No motorways or bypasses in those days.

No 51 was one of eight Leyland TB5 single-deck trolleybuses purchased in 1937 with a Brush 32-seat centre-entrance body. It is seen in 1950 at Market Place (the A1 is in the background behind No 51). It is loading for Neasham Road (route 3) which was linked with Faverdale (note the offside blind).
C. Carter

St Helens

Left: St Helens introduced trolleybuses in 1927 and by 1938 had about 56 vehicles in service on eight routes. Other than the first 10, all trolleybuses were lowbridge double-deck examples with 50 seats, or in the case of the five three-axle Ransomes, 60 seats. In 1942 St Helens received a batch of 10 8ft-wide Sunbeam MF2 trolleybus chassis intended for Johannesburg in South Africa. These became the only 8ft lowbridge double-deck trolleybuses to operate in Britain. A further 10 utility type W4 Sunbeams fitted with Roe 7ft 6in-wide bodies arrived in 1945. In 1950/51 16 highbridge-bodied trolleybuses arrived with East Lancs bodies, eight being Sunbeam type F4 and the other eight being the first BUT 961T type chassis to be ordered. The bodies for the Sunbeams were built by East Lancs (Bridlington) Ltd. No 381, one of the Sunbeams, is seen in 1956 at Prescot on route 7. *R. Brook*

Below left: No 386, one of the BUT trolleybuses, is seen approaching Prescot in 1956. *R. Brook*

Right: In Ormskirk Street, St Helens, one could see a variety of trolleybuses. In 1956 South Lancs No 4, a 1930 Guy BTX, is working the joint service to Atherton; one of the 1945 St Helens utility-bodied Sunbeam trolleybuses, No 312, is loading for Haydock; whilst Sunbeam F4 No 376 overtakes on its way to Prescot. The last St Helens trolleybus ran in 1958, while South Lancs withdrew its last routes on 31 August 1958. *R. Brook*

South Lancs

Left: South Lancashire Transport Co introduced trolleybuses in 1930 and operated them until 1958. A network of services connected St Helens to Atherton, Leigh to Bolton, and Farnworth to Atherton by a circuitous route 14 miles long linking the two termini, which were only 5 miles apart. The total route mileage was over 30 miles and the company only ever possessed 71 trolleybuses. The first 46 were Guy BT or BTX trolleybuses all with lowbridge Roe bodies. The first highbridge trolleybuses arrived in 1935, so by 1939 one Guy and 12 Leyland three-axle examples were in the fleet. During the war six two-axle utility-bodied Karrier W4 trolleybuses arrived. The last vehicles to be purchased arrived in 1947/48 and were Karrier MS2 trolleybuses. No 59, the last prewar Leyland TTB4 to be delivered, is seen in Bolton in 1949 still sporting its grey roof. *C. Carter*

Above: No 68, one of the six Karrier MS2 Weymann-bodied trolleybuses, is seen in Atherton on its way to Leigh in 1956. *R. Brook*

Brighton, Hove & District

Above: In December 1937 Brighton, Hove & District Omnibus Co Ltd, a subsidiary company of Thomas Tilling Ltd, entered into an agreement with Brighton Corporation to co-ordinate transport in the area using motor and trolleybuses. This agreement stated that the company would provide one-fifth of the trolleybus rolling stock and pay the Corporation for the use of the overhead equipment and power used. The initial company fleet of eight trolleybuses had the same livery as the Corporation ones. Both carried Brighton, Hove & District Transport lettering, with the Corporation's crest appearing on the 44 Corporation vehicles. Both fleets had the AEC 661T two-axle model with Crompton Parkinson motors and Allan West electrical equipment (made in Brighton). Whilst the Corporation chose Weymann metal-framed bodies, the company's ones were composite (in line with the group's bus bodies of the period). The war caused the full scheme to be delayed until the return to peacetime conditions. So the company's eight trolleybuses were stored until 1944, when they were moved to the Corporation's depot in Lewes Road, two entering service in November 1944 and three in January 1945, the other three following in 1945/46. In February 1946 the company's trolleybuses moved into their own depot prior to the additional routes commencing in March 1946 linking Seven Dials to Black Rock. This BH&D trolleybus (344 CPM 101), is seen outside the company's Whitehawk garage, which was the only one in the original Tilling group, which sold out to the British Transport Commission in 1948, to have accommodated trolleybuses. *Courtesy Photobus*

Hastings

Below: In 1928 trolleybuses started replacing trams in Hastings and by 1931 a fleet of 58 Guy BTX three-axle trolleybuses were in use. Fifty of these were single-deckers with Ransomes bodies, the other eight being open-top double-deck vehicles with Dodson bodies. In 1940 the first of the replacement fleet of 45 double-deck trolleybuses arrived, the last ones arriving in 1948. The first 20 were AEC type 661T chassis with Weymann or Park Royal bodies, the last 25 being Sunbeam W4 chassis with similar bodies from the same body builders. No 41, one of the Weymann-bodied Sunbeams, is seen in 1950 proudly displaying the Hastings Tramways Company fleet name which was used until 1957, when the company was absorbed by Maidstone & District Motor Services which had acquired the company in 1935. In 1959 the trolleybuses were replaced in the interests of integration by M&D motorbus services. *C. Carter*

Cleethorpes

Left: In 1936 Cleethorpes Urban District Council acquired the interests in Cleethorpes of the Great Grimsby Street Tramways Co and after a change in status became a Corporation from November 1936. In July 1937 Cleethorpes introduced 10 new trolleybuses as its share of a joint route linking Cleethorpes with Grimsby which was jointly worked with Grimsby Corporation. Cleethorpes 52 is seen in 1952 at the Grimsby Old

Market Place terminus. It was new in 1937 and had a 56-seat Park Royal body mounted on its AEC 661T chassis. *C. Carter*

Above: After the war Cleethorpes purchased six further trolleybuses. No 62 was one of the four BUT 9611T examples purchased in 1950 with Northern Coach Builders 54-seat bodies. It is seen in 1955 passing the Grimsby depot. *R. Brook*

Grimsby

Above: Grimsby Corporation introduced single-deck Garrett trolleybuses on a route linking Riby Square to Weelsby Road in 1926 and purchased a further two Garretts in 1927. In 1936 10 three-axle AEC 664T Roe-bodied double-deckers with centre entrances were purchased for the intended joint route to Cleethorpes. In 1956 Grimsby No 17 is seen at the Old Market Place on a short working to the Grimsby boundary at Park Street. One of the two Roe-bodied Crossley trolleybuses owned by Cleethorpes is seen behind No 17. *R. Brook*

Grimsby-Cleethorpes Transport

Right: On 1 January 1957 the transport departments of the two adjoining towns of Grimsby and Cleethorpes came under the control of a joint committee which introduced a new blue and cream livery to replace the former liveries. One of the six former Grimsby 1947 Karrier W4 chassis with Roe 56-seat bodies is seen outside the former Grimsby depot which had become the base for all the vehicles for the joint committee. The Cleethorpes vehicles had 100 added to the former fleetnumber to prevent duplication. The remaining route was discontinued in 1960. *G. Lumb*

TRADES CLUB

FB-5570

Mexborough & Swinton

Left: When Mexborough & Swinton Tramways Co introduced trolleybuses in August 1915 it was the second of the companies in which the National Electric Construction Co Ltd had a financial interest to do so. The first one had been Rhondda Tramways Co Ltd in late 1914. In 1929, after the withdrawal of the last trams which had been replaced by more trolleybuses, the company changed its name to the M&S Traction Co. In 1931 the British Electric Traction Co Ltd gained control of the NECC Ltd and its subsidiaries.

To replace earlier vehicles six secondhand ones were purchased in 1937 from Notts & Derby, one of the Balfour Beatty subsidiary companies. One of these, No 66 (RB 5570), had been built in 1931 and was one of the last batch of English Electric-designed and built single-deck trolleybuses. It originally entered service on 7 January 1932 and was withdrawn from service in July 1950. *C. Carter*

Brighton

Above: Brighton Corporation introduced trolleybuses between 1 May and 1 September 1939, with the other routes and extensions being delayed until the war was over. The remaining routes were built in 1946 and then in 1948–1951 various extensions were added. Brighton Corporation trolleybuses were similar to the ones provided by the Brighton, Hove & District Co except that the coat of arms was carried by the Corporation ones. The first routes to be withdrawn in 1959 enabled the company vehicles to be taken out of service and the remaining routes continued to operate until 30 June 1961. Typical of the final year is this scene near Preston Park where the 46A joined the 46 route from Hollingbury before returning via Beaconsfield Villas to the Aquarium and Old Steine. No 27 (FUF 27) is seen working the anti-clockwise Preston Circle route 26A which then returned as the 46A. *G. Lumb*

London

Left: The largest trolleybus system in the world was constructed between 1935 and 1941 in London when many of the tram routes were converted to trolleybus operation. Some 250 route miles were involved; these were in addition to the small system operated by London United in the southwest suburbs around Kingston where 60 trolleybuses had been introduced in 1931. In 1933 these had come under the control of the London Passenger Transport Board. The LPTB introduced some 1,700 new trolleybuses to operate these new services. The orders for these had been placed with Leyland, which supplied 864 vehicles, 427 of which had Leyland bodies, and AEC, which supplied the balance either on conventional three-axle chassis or embodying an AEC-patented unit construction, where the chassis frame was considerably lighter than usual and incorporated cross-members and outriggers to coincide with the side pillars of the bodywork. The balance of AEC type vehicles were built by MCCW where the bodybuilder constructed a metal-framed body to which the AEC axles and running units were fitted, Met-Cam supplying 175 of these. During the war London received 43 three-axle trolleybuses intended for export to South Africa, since due to the high risk of loss at sea of merchant shipping to the German U-boats, these were not shipped. After the war London's remaining tram routes were converted to motorbus operation and only 127 BUT 9641T trolleybuses were purchased to replace the original 60 London United and other early vehicles. Abandonment was swift, with the main system closing between 1959 and 8 May 1962. The variety of vehicles is so wide that the author has limited his choice to just three over the following pages.

The first stage of abandonment included the isolated Bexleyheath routes and the Sutton to Crystal Palace route, No 654, which used the oldest vehicles. Our view shows one of the 1935 Leyland TTB2 chassis fitted with a body built by the Birmingham Railway Carriage & Wagon Co. These early vehicles were only some 27ft long and seated 60. One of class B1, No 85 (CGF 85), is seen near West Croydon in about 1954, when roads were not gridlocked, on its way from Crystal Palace to Sutton. *R. Brook*

Below: Typical of the 175 chassisless trolleybuses using AEC running units is No 1428 (FXH 428), which was one of the largest single batch of identical class L3 vehicles, Nos 1380–1529, built by MCCW (Metro-Cammell Carriage and Wagon Works) and delivered new between August 1939 and June 1940. No 1428 is seen heading to Holborn from North Finchley on route 517 in the mid-1950s. *R. Brook*

Above: The last batch of prewar standard London trolleybuses to be delivered were the batch of 25 class P1 vehicles delivered between January 1941 and October 1941. These were also the last Leyland LPTB70 chassis to be built. No 1701 (GGP 701) is seen turning at West Croydon for its return journey to Harlesden on route 630. For many years route 630 had its northern terminus displayed as Nr Willesden Junction on the destination blinds. This was also London's longest route, being 14.67 miles long, a few hundred yards longer than Notts & Derby and South Lancs routes.

R. Brook

Portsmouth

Above: Portsmouth introduced trolleybuses in 1934 when a mixed bag of 15 vehicles from four chassis manufacturers entered service on a route linking South Parade Pier to Cosham. The four three-axle examples did not get approval and for the next route nine AEC type 661T chassis with English Electric bodies arrived in 1935. Satisfied with these, orders were placed for a further 76 AEC type 661T trolleybuses. This time the only body builder willing to build 76 identical bodies in one batch was Craven, which delivered them during 1936 and 1937. Five of these AEC 661T chassis with Craven 52-seat bodies are seen at the Dockyard terminus in 1961 on route 12 to Green Lane and routes 17 & 18 to Eastney and Milton. *G. Lumb*

Above: The only postwar trolleybuses to be purchased by Portsmouth were 15 BUT 9611T chassis with 52-seat Burlingham bodies which entered service in 1950/51. One of these, No 308 (ERV 933), is seen on route 6 which linked Cosham to Dockyard via Eastney, South Parade Pier and Southsea. The outward route was numbered 5 in line with the policy used by Portsmouth which allocated two numbers to each route. Incidentally, service 5/6 was the last trolleybus route to operate in Portsmouth when withdrawn on 27 July 1963. *G. Lumb*

Ipswich

Below: In 1923 Ipswich introduced three hired trolleybuses on an experimental route from the main railway station to the Cornhill in the town centre. They were successful and further single-deck trolleybuses were purchased until 1933 when the first double-deck trolleybuses appeared. By 1939 Ipswich had purchased 66 out of the 86 trolleybuses operated from the local manufacturer Ransomes, Sims & Jeffries, with a further 16 being purchased from Garrett, another East Anglian supplier. The last Ransomes trolleybus to be supplied to a British operator had arrived in 1939. A further 40 trolleybuses arrived between 1944 and 1950; these were from Karrier or Sunbeam. One of the last 12 Sunbeams, No 116, supplied new in 1950, is seen in 1951 with the upper and lower deck side panels having the surface burnished instead of painted, on the Park Royal-built body.
C. Carter

Above: The last batch of Karrier-'badged' trolleybuses to be built entered service at Ipswich in early 1949. One of these, No 112, is seen in 1961 on a wet day working route 3 which linked Witton (Norwich Road) with Rushmere Heath. *G. Lumb*

Doncaster

Right: Doncaster converted its Bentley tram route to trolleybus operation in August 1928 using six-wheel double-deck Garrett and Karrier-Clough chassis, fitted with Roe 60-seat bodies. Further routes were converted during 1929/31 using more Karrier-Cloughs fitted with Roe bodies. Doncaster also placed into service one of the two trolleybuses built by Bristol Tramways & Carriage Co which became fleetnumber 31.

After Clough, Smith & Co ceased to act as sole agent for the supply of the Karrier-Clough trolley omnibuses in March 1933, Doncaster was one of the first customers to purchase direct from Karrier Motors Ltd. The chassis of No 32 was displayed at the 1933 Commercial Motor Show and was then fitted with a new Roe body before entering service in January 1934. In 1947 it was renumbered 332 and this 1951 view shows it loading at Doncaster North Bridge before leaving on route 1 to Bentley, which in 1956 was the first service to be abandoned. No 332 was withdrawn in May 1952 after Doncaster purchased six BUT double-deck trolleybuses built in 1949 from Darlington.

C. Carter

Left: Doncaster had received a number of utility Karrier type W4 trolleybuses during the war. To replace the remaining Karrier three-axle trolleybuses, a further eight secondhand ones were purchased from Southend in 1954. This also enabled Doncaster to rebody its own utility vehicles as well as further secondhand chassis before rebodying the Southend vehicles. No 391 was placed back into service in September 1958, with the last rebodied vehicle entering service in May 1959. Out of the 28 rebodied Sunbeam/Karrier trolleybuses, 20 of the Roe bodies were transferred to either new or refurbished motorbus chassis when the system

closed between 1961 and 1963. No 391 is seen at Hexthorpe in 1960. After withdrawal from service, the bodies from 20 of Doncaster's 28 rebodied trolleybuses were transferred to existing or new motorbus chassis. In April 1974, when South Yorkshire PTE took over the operations of Doncaster Corporation and more than two years after the last trolleybus ran in Bradford, 13 of these were still in service. *G. Lumb*

South Shields
Above: South Shields operated trolleybuses between October 1936 and April 1964. Its prewar fleet comprised 34 two-axle Karrier E4

trolleybuses with Weymann bodies, and the prototype Willowbrook-bodied Daimler trolleybus. During the war secondhand vehicles were purchased from Bournemouth and Bradford. Typical of the 34 Karriers was fleet No 212, new in 1938. It is seen in 1960 approaching the roundabout at Chichester on its way back to the Market from Tyne Dock and Stanhope Road. The bamboo trolley pole used by the conductor to retrieve the trolleys in the event of a dewirement is seen in its mountings above the lower saloon windows. *G. Lumb*

Above: The postwar fleet at South Shields included 23 Northern Coach Builders-bodied two-axle Karrier W4 and F4 chassis. The last ones were delivered with Sunbeam badges after Rootes had sold Sunbeam Commercial Vehicles Ltd to Brockhouse, which then resold it in 1948 to Guy Motors Ltd after the company's name had been changed to the Sunbeam Trolleybus Co. Rootes retained the 'Karrier' name for use on the commercial vehicles it was still producing for the local authority users. Three of the 1947 examples are shown in 1963 at the Market. The first vehicle, No 256, is not going anywhere yet! Look at where the trolleys are resting! *G. Lumb*

Kingston upon Hull

Right: Hull operated trolleybuses between 25 July 1937 and 31 October 1964, the fleet reaching a peak of 100 vehicles in 1948. All trolleybuses had Metropolitan-Vickers electrical equipment and only two-axle models were bought. No 28 (ERH 28) is seen in June 1960 at Newlands Avenue on route 62. This was one of 20 Crossley type TDD4 vehicles placed into service in 1938. The body was built by Cravens. *G. Lumb*

Below right: A further 20 Leyland TB7 trolleybuses arrived in 1939. This time the body builder was East Lancs. No 63 (FRH 563) is seen in June 1960 on Holderness Road. *G. Lumb*

Left: At the 1952 Commercial Motor Show Mr G. H. Pulfrey, the enterprising General Manager at Hull, displayed a revolutionary trolleybus for Britain. This was a Sunbeam MF2B chassis fitted with a forward-entrance/centre-exit 54-seat body built by Roe. This was placed into service in January 1953 and was fleet number 101. It was the first example of this type of vehicle to be placed into service in Britain; a further 15 were delivered in 1954/55 and these were known as the 'Coronation' type. It had been Mr Pulfrey's intention to use them for one-man-operation and, as a result, all were fitted with trolley retrievers, making them the most advanced trolleybuses to be used in Britain. No 101 is seen at Cottingham Road Garage in August 1964 and was the last trolleybus to operate, on the evening of 31 October 1964. *G. Lumb*

Rotherham
Above: In 1912 Rotherham introduced trolleybuses linking the Herringthorpe Lane tram terminus with Maltby some seven miles from Rotherham. In January 1924 the service was extended into Rotherham enabling a through service to operate to the town centre from Maltby. In 1949–51 44 new Daimler three-axle single-deck trolleybuses were placed into service fitted with East Lancs 38-seat centre-entrance bodies. No 11 (FET 611) was one of the last batch to enter service and is seen in 1955 leaving the town centre for Silverwood. In 1956/57 it was one of 20 to be rebuilt and fitted with new double-deck bodies. No 11 then became fleetnumber 41. *R. Brook*

Above: One of the rebuilt and rebodied Daimler trolleybuses, No 35, is seen at Kimberworth terminus in 1961 before returning to Thryburgh. No 35 was one of the 20 single-deck trolleybuses to receive a new 70-seat Roe body in 1956/57. It had originally been single-deck No 78. The remaining routes at Rotherham using these double-deck-bodied trolleybuses were converted to motorbus operation between 1963 and October 1965. *G. Lumb*

Nottingham
Right: Between 10 April 1927 and 30 June 1966 trolleybuses operated in Nottingham. Nottingham 476 (HAU 176) was one of 10 Park Royal-bodied Karrier W4 trolleybuses delivered in 1946.
G. Lumb

Left: Nottingham only operated 30 8ft-wide trolleybuses. Five Sunbeams had been acquired in 1942 when wartime problems prevented them being shipped to South Africa. A further 25 were placed into service in 1949/50; these were BUT type 9641T and had 70-seat Brush bodies. White steering wheels were fitted to remind the driver that the vehicle was 8ft wide and they could be used only on designated routes approved by the Ministry of Transport. No 513 (KTV 513) is seen at Carlton on the cross-town route 39. The driver has also taken the precaution of placing a chock in front of the offside wheel after leaving the cab to join the conductor for a break. *G. Lumb*

Newcastle

Above right: Trolleybuses served the city and county of Newcastle upon Tyne from 1 October 1935 to 1 October 1966. The first postwar order for trolleybuses Newcastle placed was with Karrier Motors Ltd for 35 two-axle, 56-seat MCCW-bodied Karrier F4 vehicles. These entered service in late 1948 or early 1949 and due to change in ownership of the trolleybus interests of Rootes, carried Sunbeam badges instead of Karrier. Again, being 8ft wide, they were confined, until the 1950 change of legislation, to specifically approved routes. No 465 is seen in March 1963 at Church Street, Walker, before returning across the city to the Brighton Grove terminus of route 35A. *G. Lumb*

Lower right: For routes where 8ft-wide trolleybuses were not acceptable (pre-1950) Newcastle ordered the first 30 examples of the new S7 model, 7ft 6in wide, from Sunbeam, this time purchasing the 70-seat bodies from Northern Coach Builders whose works were in the city. No 527, new in January 1949, is seen in 1961 with the driver giving a hand signal that he is pulling out from the kerb in Northumberland Street. *G. Lumb*

Left: Fifty two-axle 7ft 6in-wide trolleybuses were also purchased, all with Northern Coach Builders 56-seat bodies, the chassis order being split equally between BUT and Sunbeam. Typical of these is No 551, one of the Sunbeam F4 examples, which is seen in March 1963 at the Wellbeck Road terminus of route 35. The Tyne shipyards can be seen in the background, whilst Jarrow church is also pictured. *G. Lumb*

SHMD

Right: When the Stalybridge, Hyde, Mossley & Dukinfield Transport and Electricity Board obtained trolleybus powers in 1936 it entered into through-running arrangements with its neighbouring authorities of Manchester and Ashton-under-Lyne for them to operate the two routes involved, whilst it maintained the overhead within its boundaries. It chose not to operate its own trolleybuses. For this concession SHMD became the sole operator of motorbuses on route 21 into Manchester. On 30 December 1966 the trolleybuses ceased to operate under its overhead and the Board's tower-wagons and linesmen became redundant. A SHMD Thornycroft tower-wagon is seen in Manchester Road, Hyde in 1963 while linesmen repair the overhead.
V. Nutton, courtesy Geoff Lumb collection

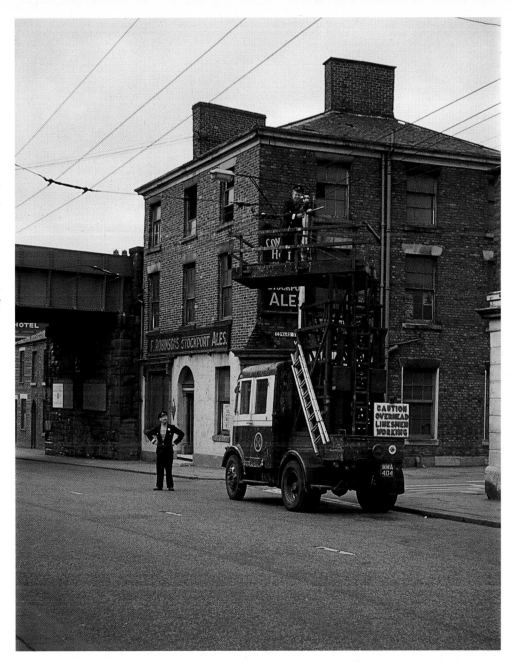

Manchester

Left: Despite opposition from the General Manager, Manchester Corporation introduced trolleybuses to the city in March 1938, using two-axle vehicles for the through routes to Stalybridge and three-axle vehicles for the short workings. Further routes followed. The last examples of the prewar trolleybuses survived until 1960. One of these two-axle Crossley TDD4s, No 1174, with

54-seat body new in November 1942, was seen on learner duties a few weeks before withdrawal in June 1960, on the turning loop at Denton, Crown Point used for the short workings on the Hyde Gee Cross route. *G. Lumb*

Above: The planned conversion of the Hyde route for September 1939 was postponed due to the outbreak of World War 2, and was delayed

until January 1950, when a new fleet of Crossley trolleybuses became available. The Manchester terminus was at George Street, Piccadilly, and at Hyde the service was extended to Gee Cross to cater for local passengers. In 1956 the Piccadilly terminus was changed to the Queen's Hotel, and this view shows both types of Crossley trolleybuses introduced in 1950 at the original George Street terminus. *R. Brook*

Ashton

Above: The trolleybus was first introduced at Ashton in 1926 when a joint service with Oldham was inaugurated. In 1938 Ashton joined with Manchester in providing new services, some being operated by arrangement for SHMD. Typical of the prewar fleet is No 49, built in 1936 as the prototype two-axle Crossley trolleybus, with Crossley 54-seat body, Ashton purchasing it in 1937. In 1955 it is seen leaving Manchester on route 219 to Ashton via Guide Bridge; 49 was withdrawn in 1956. *R. Brook*

Right: The joint routes to Stalybridge often meant that if a breakdown occurred, the vehicle was recovered by the nearest depot. In 1960 one of Manchester's BUTs had been taken to Ashton's Mossley Road garage. It is seen with one of the last two 1940 Ashton Crossleys, which survived until 1965. Both vehicles are parked with the front wheels chocked to prevent them running away. Trolleybuses continued to run until 30 December 1966. *G. Lumb*

Wolverhampton

Left: Wolverhampton's first trolleybuses were introduced in October 1923. From 1926 all trolleybuses purchased had chassis built in Wolverhampton by either Guy Motors Ltd or Sunbeam Commercial Vehicles Ltd. Typical of the postwar purchases is Sunbeam F4 No 617 with a 8ft-wide Park Royal 54-seat body. One of the 1949 Guy BT chassis, with similar bodywork, is seen in the background in this 1963 scene at Victoria Square, Wolverhampton. The white steering wheels were fitted to identify the 8ft-wide vehicles. *G. Lumb*

Above: In 1959 a new livery was introduced for Wolverhampton's trolleybuses, but after six had been repainted into a dark blue-green livery with a straw-coloured waistband, the policy was changed and the former green and primrose livery reappeared. One of the six, No 471, is seen at the Wednesfield Albion Inn terminus, whilst one of the earlier Sunbeam W4 trolleybuses, No 433, rebodied by Roe in September 1959, is operating an enthusiasts' special tour on Sunday 19 May 1963. The Wolverhampton system finally closed on 5 March 1967. *G. Lumb*

Maidstone

Left: In 1928 Maidstone introduced trolleybuses and it took until 1963 for the system to reach its maximum route mileage of just over seven miles. The last new trolleybuses purchased by Maidstone were the 12 Sunbeam W4 chassis with 56-seat Northern Coach Builders bodies new in 1946/47. One of these, No 71, new in April 1947, is seen in 1961 at the Bull Inn, Barming waiting to depart to Parkwood. Again the driver has placed his chock in front of the offside wheel to prevent early departure without him! *G. Lumb*

Right: In June 1963, Maidstone No 85, one of five secondhand Sunbeam W4 trolleybuses purchased from Maidstone & District Motor Services after their Hastings system closed in 1959, is seen in Tonbridge Road on its way to Barming. The Corporation depot is on the left beyond the zebra crossing. *G. Lumb*

Glasgow

Left: Glasgow introduced trolleybuses in April 1949 and did not open its last route until 1958. The system then declined from 1959 until closure on 27 May 1967. The first 34 BUT type 9641T trolleybuses, Nos TB1–34, were introduced in 1949 and were identical to the London Transport Q1-type vehicles, supplied with MCCW bodies. In 1951 TB9 still carried the London Transport trolleybus transfer on the front dash panel when seen crossing Albert Bridge on its way to Shawfield. *C. Carter*

Below left: By 1955, when TB23 was seen on learner duties, the livery had been changed and, after protests from London Transport, the trolleybus transfers had disappeared. The front dash panel shows lack of care by the drivers when stopping. *R. Brook*

Right: When R. Brook photographed TB78 when new, he was not aware that it would operate a special five-hour tour on the last day of operation of Glasgow trolleybuses, after which TB78 was purchased for preservation. It can be seen at Sandtoft Transport Centre. TB78 was one of the 90 BUT 9613T chassis built with Crossley bodies. They were supplied in 1958/9 and enabled the last major expansion, the $9^1/_2$-mile-long 106 route, linking Millerston or Riddrie with Bellahouston, to be converted from tramcar operation on 15 June 1958. *R. Brook*

Above: The last route to be converted from tram to trolleybus operation, on 15 November 1958, was route 108 from Mount Florida to Paisley Road Toll which was extended at peak hours westwards to Linthouse and Shieldhall. Special dispensation was obtained by the Glasgow manager, Mr E. R. L. Fitzpayne to operate experimentally high-capacity single-deck trolleybuses 35ft long, and 10 BUT RETB1 chassis, with 50-seat Burlingham bodies, arrived in late 1958 to operate this route. Its successful operation paved the way for the general use of 36ft-long vehicles from 1961. The last of the 10, TBS21, is seen in April 1962 at Paisley Road Toll. TBS21 also survived into preservation. *G. Lumb*

Derby

Right: Derby operated trolleybuses between 9 January 1932 and 9 September 1967. Its initial fleet comprised three-axle Guys with Brush bodies. These were followed by four three-axle vehicles for comparative trials from Karrier, Ransomes, Sunbeam and Thornycroft, none of which gained favour. After further Guys, six two-axle Daimler trolleybuses arrived in 1938. Derby had to wait until 1945 for its first Ministry of War allocation of new trolleybuses. The first of these, No 171, one of two with Weymann utility bodies on Sunbeam W4 chassis, is seen outside Ascot Drive depot in March 1964, with one of the 1949 Brush-bodied Sunbeam F4 trolleybuses behind. *G. Lumb*

Above: After ordering a further 20 Sunbeam F4 trolleybuses with Brush bodies, Derby found that its order was transferred from Brush to Willowbrook when the latter took over its bodybuilding activities in 1952, the first of the 20 being completed by Willowbrook in late 1952.

The last one, No 235, entered service in March 1953; it is seen in June 1962. No 235 was the last Sunbeam F4 built and it appears that these 20 are the only Sunbeam F4 models built with 27ft-long double-deck bodies after the 1951 change in permitted length. *G. Lumb*

Belfast

Below: In 1950 a further 24 BUT type 9641T trolleybuses, again with
Harkness 68-seat bodies, were ordered, but due to delays in building bus
bodies, the chassis had to be stored until 1953. No 211 was the first one to
enter service in October 1954. One of these, No 224, is seen in July 1964
passing Falls Park on Falls Road route 12.
V. Nutton, courtesy Geoff Lumb collection

Left: In 1958 Belfast took delivery of its last new trolleybus, No 246. It was a two-axle Sunbeam type F4A, 30ft long, with a 68-seat Harkness body. It was intended to be the prototype vehicle for a new fleet which did not materialise, due to the rapid decline in trolleybus operators from the late 1950s. It is seen in July 1964 at Glen Road terminus on route 13, before returning on route 18 to Fort William on Shore Road.
V. Nutton, courtesy Geoff Lumb collection

Huddersfield

Below: On 4 December 1933 Huddersfield introduced trolleybuses on an experimental route to Almondbury, using six vehicles from four suppliers. Satisfied with this improved form of transport, the majority of the tram routes were converted between 1934 and 1940. When the fleet reached its maximum size, only three of the 140 trolleybuses were not supplied by Karrier Motors, which until 1935 had been a major employer in Huddersfield. After

Humber Ltd (a part of Rootes Securities) took over the company in 1934, trolleybus manufacture was moved to the Sunbeam factory in Wolverhampton. Typical of the prewar Huddersfield trolleybuses was the batch of 85 Karriers supplied in 1938. This one, seen parked in St George's Square in 1954, was one of the 65 bodied by Park Royal; both Brush and Weymann each bodied 10 similar vehicles. The seating capacity was 64.
R. Brook

Left: The first postwar fleet replacements arrived between 1947 and 1949 and comprised 52 Park Royal-bodied type MS2 trolleybuses, this time with 70 seats. The first 28 carried Karrier badges and the other 24 had Sunbeam badges; this was because Rootes had sold the trolleybus business of both Karrier and Sunbeam to Brockhouse in 1946, with the Karrier name being retained by Rootes for use on the commercial vehicles supplied mainly for local authority users. No 543, one of the Karrier-badged MS2 trolleybuses, is seen in 1955 approaching Huddersfield on its way from Longwood to Brighouse. On 9 July 1955 the part of the route outside the Borough of Huddersfield from Fixby to Brighouse was converted to motorbuses, after only 15 years' operation. *R. Brook*

Above: When economies started dictating purchasing policies after the nationalisation of the electricity generators, Huddersfield, like many other users, rebodied existing chassis to prolong their life. No 493 was the first one of 28 Karrier type E6 trolleybuses to be rebodied with 66-seat Roe bodies between 1950 and 1954. On 1 October 1961 No 493 was hired by the author for the first trolleybus tour of the Huddersfield system. It is seen at the Slaithwaite turning loop on its way to Marsden which was the longest route, extending 7½ miles up the Colne Valley from Huddersfield. *G. Lumb*

Reading

Above: Reading's first trolleybus service commenced on 18 July 1936 with six trolleybuses supplied by five manufacturers, all having lowbridge bodies built by Park Royal. In 1939 further tram routes were converted when 25 AEC type 661T trolleybuses entered service. This time, by obtaining permission to move the motor position rearwards on the AEC 661T chassis, to give the same clearance as allowed for three-axle designs, Reading was able to fit conventional highbridge bodies, 15ft 1in high, which enabled them to pass under the low bridges in the town. In 1948 Huddersfield sold 12 of its 1934 Karrier E6 trolleybuses to Reading for £200 each. Six of these were reconditioned and placed into service between September 1948 and February 1951. The first one to enter service at Reading, No 158, originally Huddersfield No 414, is seen at Whitley Wood waiting to return to Stations, a route opened on 7 August 1949.
J. Copland, courtesy R. Brook

Right: In 1949 Reading's first 20 8ft-wide trolleybuses arrived fitted with Park Royal 56-seat bodies with rear doors mounted on BUT 9611T chassis. No 145 is seen at Whitley Wood in 1961. *G. Lumb*

Left: The next new trolleybuses to be received were 12 three-axle Sunbeam S7 models with 68-seat bodies, again built by Park Royal. Park Royal had been the main body supplier since 1933 when a former General Manager of Reading, Mr G. F. Craven, became a director of Park Royal. (In late 1933 he moved again when he was appointed as General Manager of Halifax, which then became another Park Royal user.) No 177 is seen at Tilehurst in 1961. *G. Lumb*

Bournemouth

Above: On 13 May 1933 Bournemouth introduced four trolleybuses hired from three manufacturers — AEC, Sunbeam and Thornycroft — for use on a one-mile-long trial route between the Square and Westbourne. Satisfied with the results, Bournemouth replaced its trams with 102 Sunbeam MS2 trolleybuses, 96 of which had Park Royal 56-seat dual-door bodies, and these entered service between 1934 and 1936. One of these Sunbeam

MS2 trolleybuses (ALJ 980) is seen in 1961 in Holdenhurst Road, Lansdowne. Supplied in 1935 as fleetnumber 106, it had been renumbered 215 in the late 1950s. Before flashing indicators became compulsory in the 1960s many vehicles were fitted with semaphore trafficator arms; one of these is mounted on the nearside cab window pillar, apparently stuck. *G. Lumb*

Above: In 1958 three of the prewar Sunbeam MS2 trolleybuses were rebuilt and converted into 69-seat open-top vehicles for special duties and circular tours of the town for holidaymakers. One of these, No 200, is seen in June 1963 at the Pier leaving for a tour in the summer sunshine. New as No 157 (BRU 8) in April 1936, it was renumbered 200 on conversion to open top in 1956. *G. Lumb*

Right: Bournemouth was the last British operator to purchase new trolleybuses and these entered service between July and October 1962. The Weymann 65-seat bodies were mounted on Sunbeam MF2B chassis and the last four entered service in October 1962. One of these, No 298 (298 LJ), is seen in June 1963 unloading passengers at Christchurch before being driven on to the turntable in the foreground which enabled it to be turned round before returning to Bournemouth. This was the last route to close, on 20 April 1969. *G. Lumb*

Cardiff

Left: The fifth and last Welsh operator to introduce trolleybuses was Cardiff which placed 10 into service during 1942/43. These were ordered from Leyland with 70-seat Northern Counties bodies. Due to World War 2, Leyland was unable to supply the chassis and AEC was allowed to build them instead, supplying type 664T chassis. The next new vehicles to arrive in 1948 were 20 BUT type 9641T trolleybuses with 67-seat dual-door bodies built by East Lancashire Coachbuilders. One of these, No 216 (DBO 476), is seen at Pengam. In 1962 this route was cut back to the Royal Oak. *R. Brook*

Right: To enable the direct route from the Monument to the Pier Head to be converted to trolleybus operation in August 1947, Cardiff purchased seven second-hand English Electric single-deck trolleybuses built in 1930 from nearby Pontypridd. This route traversed Bute Street and went under the Great Western railway to the east of Cardiff General station. In 1949 these secondhand trolleybuses were replaced by five dual-door 38-seat East Lancs-bodied BUT 9641T single-deckers, and then in 1955 a further similar vehicle, No 243 (KBO 961), was placed in service. This carried an East Lancashire Coachbuilders 40-seat rear-entrance body and was the last three-axle single-deck trolleybus to enter service in Britain. In April 1963, No 243 is seen climbing up from the low railway bridge in Bute Street on its way to the Monument. *D. J. Smithies*

Below right: Cardiff's last new double-deck trolleybuses entered service in May 1955, when the Victoria Park route was extended to Green Farm Road and Grand Avenue at Ely. One of these, No 282, a 72-seat East Lancashire Coachbuilders body on a BUT 9641T chassis, is seen in July 1967 at the City Terminus in Wood Street, with two linesmen carrying out running repairs to the trolley booms after gaining access to the roof from the rear upper deck emergency window. Cardiff's last trolleybus ran on 11 January 1970. *G. Lumb*

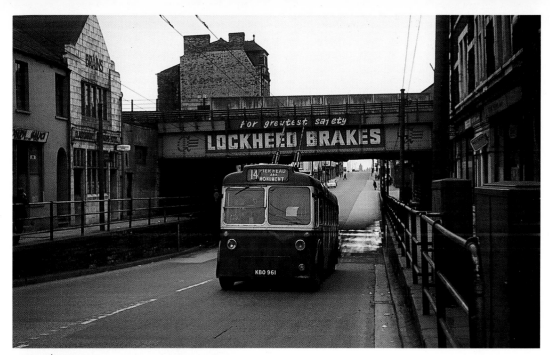

Walsall

Above: Walsall introduced four trolleybuses on the route to Willenhall in July 1931. In November 1932, to avoid changing vehicles in Willenhall, Walsall and Wolverhampton introduced a joint service linking the two towns. In 1933 a further 15 trolleybuses were placed into service on other routes. Walsall purchased its last new trolleybus in 1956 and then continued to purchase secondhand examples from Pontypridd, Hastings, Cleethorpes and Ipswich. One of the Hastings' Sunbeam type W4 trolleybuses, with Weymann 56-seat body, is seen in June 1960 at the Wolverhampton terminus of the joint route. No 305 had been Hastings No 36 when new in 1948. Wolverhampton Sunbeam No 614 is seen behind. *G. Lumb*

Right: In 1950 Walsall purchased 10 26ft-long Brush-bodied 56-seat Sunbeam F4 chassis. In June 1963 No 336, still in the earlier livery with dark blue bands, is seen loading in Walsall for Beechdale Estate, the driver having chocked the front offside wheel whilst out of the cab. *G. Lumb*

Left: On 1 October 1969, Walsall became part of the West Midlands Passenger Transport Executive, which closed the remaining routes between February 1970 and 2 October 1970. On 30 September 1969, Walsall was still training trolleybus drivers and one of the 1950 Sunbeam F4 trolleybuses, No 339, is seen on learner duties at Beechdale Estate. *D. J. Smithies*

Teesside

Right: In 1919 Teesside Railless Traction Board was formed to take over the partially completed trolleybus system built for the North Ormesby, South Bank, Normanby and Grangetown Railless Traction Co. The new Board was jointly owned by Middlesbrough Corporation with one third share and Eston Urban District Council who held the other two thirds. Services commenced on 8 November 1919 using 10 single-deck vehicles. Until 1944 only single-deck vehicles were purchased and one of the 1936 batch of Leylands has been shown earlier on page 11 at Southend. In 1944 the Ministry of War Transport allocated eight utility-bodied Sunbeam W4 trolleybuses, with Weymann and Roe each building four of the bodies. One of the first two to enter service in October 1944 was No 16, with a Weymann utility body. It is seen in April 1960 at Normanby with the driver giving a hand signal that he is turning right. *G. Lumb*

Left: In 1950 a further eight Sunbeam F4 trolleybuses arrived with attractive East Lancashire Coachbuilders (Bridlington) Ltd-built 56-seat bodies. No 2 (GAJ 12) is seen in September 1963 at North Ormesby waiting to leave for Normanby. *G. Lumb*

Above: On 31 March 1968, TRTB opened the last new trolleybus route to be built in Britain after erecting a mile of new overhead linking the two termini at Grangetown and Normanby to give a circular service. On 1 April 1968 TRTB was one of three municipalities to be merged to form Teesside Municipal Transport. The TMT chose a new livery of turquoise, instead of the blue and greens of the former fleets of Middlesbrough, Stockton and Teesside RTB. During 1969 TMT purchased five forward-entrance trolleybuses from Reading. In 1970 these were renumbered into the combined TMT fleet with a 'T' prefix. T290 (VRD 185), originally Reading No 185, is seen in late 1970 outside the South Bank depot. The Teesside trolleybuses ceased to operate public services on 4 April 1971. On 18 April 1971, a ceremonial final journey was operated using a decorated trolleybus. So ended over 52 years' operation on a system which reached a maximum route mileage of just 9.2 miles in 1968. *R. Brook*

Bradford

Left: Bradford and Leeds had both started to operate the first British trolleybus routes on 20 June 1911. In July 1928, Leeds became the seventh operator to abandon them. Bradford continued to develop its system and was able to survive until 24 March 1972, when it became the last of the 50 British trolleybus operators. In 1938/39 English Electric supplied Bradford with a large batch of 57 trolleybuses, all with English Electric traction equipment made in Bradford. Forty-two of these were English Electric-bodied AEC type 661T trolleybuses and the other 15 were Weymann-bodied Karrier type E4 chassis. One of the Karriers, No 681 (CAK 681), new in January 1939, is seen at Thornbury in May 1960. *G. Lumb*

Below left: In June 1961, Bradford celebrated 50 years of trolleybus operation by painting two vehicles in earlier liveries. No 603 (KY 8206), one of the 1934 AEC 661T trolleybuses, rebodied in 1947 with a Northern Coach Builders body, was repainted in the 1911 livery and it achieved fame in April 1962 when it completed its one millionth mile. No 687 (CAK 687), one of the 1939 Karriers, was repainted into the 1939 livery. No 787 (GHN 564), was one of the first former Darlington Karrier W4 single-deckers to be rebuilt with an East Lancashire Coachbuilders forward-entrance double-deck body in November 1958. Passing these three trolleybuses (being used for a special tour on Saturday 20 June 1961) is No 691, one of the 1939 Karriers rebodied by Crossley in 1952. *G. Lumb*

Above: The last Bradford trolleybuses to enter service were seven former Mexborough & Swinton Sunbeam F4 chassis rebuilt before they were fitted with new 66-seat East Lancashire Coachbuilders forward-entrance bodies. One of these, No 843 (FWX 913), had on 26 March 1961, after having most of its body cut down to become an open tourer, been used to carry the Rawmarsh Brass Band in the procession over the Mexborough system the day after public services ceased. It seems appropriate that, as Bradford No 843, this vehicle was to become the last trolleybus to work a

scheduled journey in Britain on 24 March 1972. It is seen at Allerton terminus, shortly before this route was withdrawn in February 1971, with Ilkley Moor in the background, and anyone familiar with the song 'Ilkley Moor Baht Hat', must appreciate that when Bradford closed in March 1972, 11 out of the 50 trolleybus systems had been in Yorkshire, and Britain was then 'Baht Trackless' for the first time in 60 years! The silent service became just silent.

G. R. Marshall, courtesy D. J. Smithies collection.